## About the Author

Vivian Johnson has published three other books. The first was, "Care Planning System for Long Term Care," which she co-authored with Helen S. Morrow, A.R.N.P., Ed.D; the second was "Zetta—The Girl Who Knew She Wanted to be a Missionary Nurse; The Lady Who Was Wise and Witty to 101" and the third, "24/7—Positive Outcomes to Critical Issues in Health Care." Vivian graduated from Moody Bible Institute in Chicago, Illinois and received her R.N. and B.S. from Montana State University, her Gerontological Nurse Practitioner certification from the University of Washington and is a state and federally licensed Administrator. Vivian's passions are two-fold: seeing that inspiration and education are a part of every encounter and every event and getting people interested in genealogy with the goal of writing their life stories. Many of the stories, Scriptures and poems in "Life's Landscape Lessons" come from Vivian's experiences as the daughter of missionary parents in Central Africa.

# Contents

# Preface

I took the classes in Joy, Trust and Hope 101 from watching and listening to my parents who, as missionaries, lived in difficult circumstances in a very primitive part of Central Africa.

The result was my love for an amazing God and His Word as well as a fascination for finding a life lesson in everything the Creator has given us.

It is my hope that these Scriptures, poems and stories which reflect my passions will, perhaps, cause you to think on the words that Elizabeth Barrett Browning penned: "Earth's crammed with heaven and every common bush afire with God, but only he who sees, takes off his shoes."

# Life's Landscape Lessons

Each year as I watch crocuses, hyacinths, daffodils and tulips push through the ground, I am reminded of how it takes the cold, hard dirt of winter to have a beautiful pageant of flowers in spring.

People of all ages can easily recall times in their lives when sorrow, hardship and pain were eased by lessons learned and the blessings they later enjoyed. And, so it is with my stories which range from being away from parents at an early age, the loss of precious family members and going without basic conveniences, only to result in rich blessings.

Having been born in a mud house in Central Africa, I spent my grade school years away from my parents at a mission school which was a five-day trip away from home. Crying myself to sleep at night from homesickness is perhaps why, today, I find myself reaching out to those who are lonely. When my doll did not arrive in our belongings from America for over a year, I made a doll by filling a hot water bottle with water, drawing a face on it, wrapping it in a towel and cuddling it—forever making me easily satisfied with whatever I have. My parents' report of how God gave them both the gift of joy in the midst of their grief while burying their toddler son in the jungles has left a deep and positive impression on my life. And, watching them kneel at the running board of our truck when faced with impossible situations and hearing their prayer that always started with, "Lord, You're our only hope," has resulted in my assurance that God is faithful. Sharing outhouses and the accompanying catalogs with lizards, caterpillars and snakes can still bring a smile of gratefulness over indoor plumbing and soft tissue! Memorizing Scripture for punishment at mission school (and I'm sorry to admit that I know the whole Bible for

*continued...*

talking in class!) has given me a life-long desire to memorize chapters of the Bible. And, flying home alone to America via Paris, wearing missionary barrel clothes was hard at the time, but it was either laugh or cry and choosing to laugh taught me the value of a sense of humor.

I have found Isaiah 61:3 to be true: "...he will give: Beauty for ashes; Joy instead of mourning; Praise instead of heaviness..." In a special dish at home, I have put petals from flowers from the most sorrowful and the most joyful occasions of life. When I lift the lid, the fragrance of all these petals together is sweet—just as life has been.

In spring as we watch the flowers burst through what was cold, hard ground, may we be reminded that it took the sorrow of our Savior's death in order to have His miraculous resurrection by which we may have eternal life.

# Oceans — Take Me To That Ocean Beach<sup>©</sup>

My favorite spot in all the world is at the ocean beach,
Where endless waves crash and spill, depositing foam at my feet.

Leave angry waves against the rocks for others to enjoy,
I'll take the waves that ebb and flow like the breath and pulse of life.

Children must love this favorite place,
where they never lack things to do,
Instead, they dig and build and collect
until they are called to go home.

And when I can no longer go or my memory begins to fade,
Help me vacation at any time by bringing that beach to me.

As I hold a delicate shell from the sea,
I'll think how it not only survived,
But how it arrived washed and polished,
with food and wonder for all.

Let that same shell bring the sound and smell of a foggy, salty coast,
While scenes of dunes and expansive beach lie before my eyes.

But whether there, or in a remembered scene,
when towards me comes that wave,
I will think of a lifetime of blessings
that have flowed from the hand of God.

Then with a mighty pull towards that horizon
which has no land in sight,
I will by faith leave that sand, defy that scary ocean
And sail to the feet of God.

# Tumbleweeds

Rootless tumbleweeds were bouncing everywhere as we drove through the desert portion of Eastern Washington to our granddaughter's state volleyball tournament.

They reminded me of the contrasting destinies of persons who are described in Jeremiah either as a rootless plant or a rooted plant.

"...Cursed is the man who puts his trust in mortal man and turns his heart away from God. He is like a stunted shrub in the desert, with no hope for the future...". (Jeremiah 17:5,6)

By contrast, Jeremiah 17:7,8 says, "But blessed is the man who trusts in the Lord and has made the Lord his hope and confidence. He is like a tree planted along a riverbank, with its roots reaching deep into the water—a tree not bothered by the heat nor worried by long months of drought. Its leaves stay green and it goes right on producing all its luscious fruit."

When we arrived at the stadium parking lot, I asked my family to catch a tumbleweed for me. It was comical watching them chase those weightless clumps of twigs that were flitting aimlessly with every breeze or the wind of a passing car.

That tumbleweed they presented to me sits on a shelf in my home. It has been used as an object lesson on many occasions and is, for me, a constant reminder of the necessity of remaining firmly planted in God's Word.

# Continental Divide

At a family camp one year, a guest speaker related how, as a boy of eight years, he made an amazing discovery. It was at the Continental Divide high in the Rocky Mountains that he found he could, with a gentle movement of his hand, move water that would have gone to the Atlantic, to the Pacific or from the Pacific, to the Atlantic.

Did it matter?  Perhaps not, but my husband and I learned as young parents that while we may not know at the moment whether a gesture, a smile or a word is either trivial or important, it just may enable a change of direction for someone at some time in the future.

While raising our daughter and son, we realized quickly that the world rewarded our children and other young people for high grades and excellence in sports.  We chose to reward them for reaching out to someone who needed a friend.  On the back of their doors was a daily checklist that started with, "Brushed teeth; Made bed..." and ended with, "Was kind to someone who needed a friend."

One day our six-year old daughter ran up the driveway, saying, "Today at school I got to choose my team.  I picked someone no one ever wants and I chose her first.  Does that count?"  With tears in my eyes, I said, "Does it ever count!"

At church when we had the opportunity to choose a Pioneer Girl Program pal, we always asked for someone who would not be chosen by others.  This was made easier because of the help of my husband who was always willing to pick up the girls who

*continued...*

had no dad, at their humble doorsteps and escort them on his arm to Father-Daughter events, as if they were his own daughter. Hopefully, that kindness, the graduation parties we gave them and the assistance in finding their first jobs, edged them into a better way of life; from the Atlantic, perhaps, to the Pacific.

# Moment Vacations

Must one leave home or exit town to experience a vacation
    Or can we find in every moment, refreshment and relaxation?
Without a single penny spent, every sense is beckoned to enjoy
    At every step, with every glance—exotic whiffs or scenes or sounds.

I close my eyes and I can relive a thousand planned vacations
    Eating papayas in morning sun as jungle songbirds serenade
    Being mesmerized by snowy peaks in our nation and abroad
    Walking the docks at Roche Harbor midst a calm, yet busy scene
    Touring with children, the USA in the bicentennial year
    Feeling the Hawaiian breeze with book and pineapple drink in hands
    Sitting beside or skiing above Priest Lake with family
    Touring the southwest canyons or meeting for reunions grand
    Experiencing travel for fun as well as genealogy
    Taking the family to London and Paris and favorite American spots,
    Relaxing on friends' deck for dinner with Italian setting and food
    Witnessing sunrise or sunset with friends at an ocean beach.

But planned vacations may be few and very far between
    So I will take a moment to study the shape of a flower
    Or communicate by squeezing a hand of an elder about to die
    Or look for meaning in clouds, whether gray or backed by blue,
    Or kiss a newborn baby's head or connect with a little child.

So put all the moments together and we will surely find
    That life is one big vacation if we'll only seize the time.

# Watchtowers

I love the Old Testament writings of the major and minor
prophets. Though they start with gloom and warning; they end
with hope because of the Promised One to come. We see in the
Book of Habakkuk that God allows us to have conversations with
Him and to even ask questions!

Habakkuk: (Habakkuk 1:2-4)
"O Lord, how long must I call for help before you will listen?...
Must I forever see this sin and sadness all around me? Wherever I
look there is oppression and bribery...The law is not enforced and
there is no justice given in the courts..."

The Lord: (Habakkuk 1:5)
"Look, and be amazed! You will be astounded at what I am about
to do! For I am going to do something in your own lifetime that
you will have to see to believe."

Habakkuk: (Habakkuk 1:12)
"O, Lord, my God, my Holy One, you who are eternal—is your
plan in all of this to wipe us out...?"

In the middle of the conversation, Habakkuk says in chapter 2,
verse 1, "I will climb my watchtower now, and wait to see what
answer God will give to my complaint."

The Lord: (Habakkuk 2:2-4)
"Write my answer on a billboard, large and clear, so that anyone
can read it at a glance and rush to tell the others...Slowly,
steadily, surely, the time approaches when the vision will be
fulfilled...for these things will surely come to pass. Just be

*continued...*

patient! They will not be overdue a single day!...the righteous man trusts in me and lives!"

Habakkuk: (Habakkuk 3:2a, 18)
"O, Lord, now I have heard your report and I worship you in awe for the fearful things you are going to do...yet I will rejoice in the Lord; I will be happy in the God of my salvation."

Have you ever climbed to the top of a mountain and found a person spending his/her summer constantly searching from the watchtower for the tiniest sign of smoke? May we be encouraged as we look out from our watchtowers as Habakkuk did, to search and find indications of God's action on our behalf and on behalf of a needy world.

# Volcanoes

My sister and I had been on a retreat at beautiful Spirit Lake at the foot of Mt. St. Helens. Our dad always said that this mountain reminded him of Mt. Fuji in its symmetry and grace.

Some participants in the retreat were late to dinner one evening. They explained that the snow cone-like mountain had beckoned them higher and higher.

Then, in May, 1980, Washington residents were reminded that this massive mountain in the Cascade Range is still an active volcano and an alert was sounded that it was waking up and could erupt at any time. Most of those living in or visiting the red zone heeded the warning. Those who did not were destroyed by the tremendous power of the volcanic blast which blew the top off and crushed whatever was in its way.

When the trembling stopped and the ash dissipated, photographers flying over the area brought back shocking pictures of former forests that looked like acres of giant matchsticks and, where Spirit Lake had been, a mud hole, void of plant or animal life.

And yet, in subsequent trips to the mountain during the years that followed, we found tiny green shoots of fir trees, emerging streams carving new pathways and, eventually, trees and wild life.

Will the God of nature not also make new life and beauty where there has been devastation in the lives of His people? Listen to Isaiah 54:10. "For the mountains may depart and the hills disappear, but my kindness shall not leave you. My promise of peace for you will never be broken, says the Lord, who has mercy upon you."

# Circles

As the Administrator, I had the unpleasant responsibility of terminating a nurse who was not safely administering medications. I had a nursing supervisor join me when we met with the employee who was accompanied by her husband, a minister. When the employee argued every point about the medication errors, her husband took out a pen and a piece of paper and drew a circle with a "10" inside of it. Around the circle, he wrote examples of people in our lives who are continually grading us, from their point of view.

He looked at his wife and said, "Honey, you are a "10" in God's eyes. With your faith in Christ, He sees you as perfect. Now, each day in our lives, people around us are grading us. As a mother, your kids would say you're about an "8"; as a driver I'd have to say you're a "2", but as a wife you're an "11!" (Now it was time for me to reach for the tissues!) At present they are saying that as an employee your grade is only a "4-5" and that's not going to do, so let's go home—we have work to do."

For years afterwards I tried to locate that couple to let them know how powerful that diagram has been in assuring individuals that in Christ, they are a "10" and no grades from others here on earth can change that.

# *Mornings*

Earlier and earlier I rise so as not to miss the dawn of a new day.
 It's not easy to leave that down pillow, but I savor being up alone.
Alone, but for the presence of the One who created daybreak.

Why can't morning last the whole day?
 Birds are cheerier, mangoes sweeter, fog horns more haunting
 in mornings.

Soft morning sun dances through my paned window, falling on
The Book opened to Isaiah:
 "I have called you by name; you are Mine; I will be with you."

Which mental and physical tasks shall I do while energy abounds—
 knowing that afternoon is on its way?

Perhaps memories of unwanted naps, goodbyes at mission school
 and sunburns cause me to not favor afternoons.
But more so, the sun doesn't dance in afternoons making me
 think that it, too, is a "Morning Person."

While sunrises seem to me a time to be alone with God,
 Sunsets are best appreciated in the company of others,
 reflecting on God's faithfulness all the hours of the day.

But, as I watch that sun disappear, I can't help being secretly
 excited that within a few hours, morning will again be here.

# Caves

At the top of our "Bucket List" was the wish to take a trip to Israel and walk where Jesus walked. Dear friends arranged for us to take that trip with them.

Many visitors to the Holy Land are disappointed at how commercialized many things are, but we were profoundly moved to be in the places where Jesus had walked, taught and healed, and died and rose again.

Qumran is a desert plateau about a mile in from the northwestern shore of the Dead Sea. This is where, in the spring of 1947, Bedouin goat herders discovered the first of the caves wherein were hidden the jars containing ancient scrolls.

Sitting on a ledge overlooking the cave where the Isaiah scrolls were found, I felt my heart pounding as I recalled how precious and how pivotal to my parents' lives and my birth, were the words of Isaiah. My mother had been undecided as to whether to deliver me at our mud house at Zemio in French Equatorial Africa (now Central Africa Republic) with the assistance of a French physician who promised to remain in the area until my birth, or to make the five-day trip to the mission doctor in the Belgian Congo. She made the decision after she and my father read the promise in Isaiah: "And I will pour out my Spirit and my blessings on your children." (Isaiah 44:3). I was born in the mud house and every birthday of my life, thereafter, mother reminded me of that verse, to which I would reply, "Yes, it has come true; I have been blessed."

I had actually seen the Dead Sea Scrolls when they were exhibited in Seattle, Washington. With a great love for God's Word and a

*continued...*

passion for genealogy, I was delighted to find the translation on a nearby wall of the words from Psalm 119 that I was looking at under glass. "Forever, O Lord, your Word stands firm in heaven. Your faithfulness extends to every generation..." (Psalm 119:89-90)

# Reflected Light

Robert Fulghum, author of *It Was on Fire When I Lay Down on It*, 1989,
Penguin Random House Publishers* asked of a Greek professor,
Dr. Papaderos, "What is the meaning of life?" to which Dr.
Papaderos replied, "I will answer your question." Taking his wallet
out of his hip pocket, he fished into a leather billfold and brought
out a very small round mirror, about the size of a quarter. "When
I was a child, during the war, we were very poor and we lived in a
remote village. One day, on the road, I found the broken pieces
of a mirror. A German motorcycle had been wrecked in that
place. I tried to find all the pieces and put them together, but it
was not possible, so I kept only the largest piece. This one. And
by scratching it on a stone I made it round. I began to play with
it as a toy and became fascinated by the fact that I could reflect
light into dark places where the sun would never shine—in deep
holes and crevices and dark closets. It became a game for me to
get light into the most inaccessible places I could find. I kept the
little mirror, and as I went about my growing up, I would take it
out in idle moments and continue the challenge of the game. As
I became a man, I grew to understand this was not just a child's
game, but a metaphor for what I might do with my life. I came
to understand that I am not the light or the source of light. But
light—truth, understanding, knowledge—is there, and it will only
shine in many dark places if I reflect it."

So impressed was I with that story, I purchased copies of the
book for staff and ordered a small mirror for each of the 65
staff member to keep on their desks or their carts as a reminder
of the privilege we have to reflect God's light into dark places or
needy lives.

*Used by permission

continued...

"For you are the Fountain of life; our light is from your Light."
(Psalm 36:9)

"But we Christians have no veil over our faces; we can be mirrors
that brightly reflect the glory of the Lord.  And as the Spirit of the
Lord works within us, we become more and more like him.  (II
Corinthians 3:18)

# Mud or Stars

"Two men looked out from the same prison bars;
One saw mud, the other stars."
(Variant of a famous proverb often attributed to Frederick
Langbridge.)

Those two men had a choice of where to focus their gaze and
therefore, their thoughts. We all have that privilege.

When we took our daughter's family to London and Paris, we
wondered how receptive our teenage grandson and granddaughter
would be to the history, the architecture and the museums. We
were pleasantly surprised that instead of their looking down with
boredom, with their digital cameras in hand, they saw everything as
something to be observed, captured and enjoyed.

We have a friend who is an exceptional photographer. She is
another example of one who looks for stars instead of mud. She's
there at sunrise, sunset and any hours in between to record scenes
in God's creation that she feels will lift others. These photos are
sent daily to friends, accompanied by an inspirational quote so
that we too, can be reminded that "The heavens are telling the
glory of God; they are a marvelous display of his craftsmanship.
Day and night they keep on telling about God. Without a sound
or word, silent in the skies, their message reaches out to all the
world." (Psalm 19: 1-4a)

Looking upward reminds me of C. S. Lewis' quote: "Aim at heaven
and you will get earth thrown in. Aim at earth and you get neither."

# Ruins

We visited three cities on our tour of Israel that Jesus prophesied would be destroyed because of the peoples' unbelief, in spite of the miracles and teachings He did in those places. As predicted, Capernum, Bethsaida and Chorazin were all destroyed. In Capernum by the Sea of Galilee where Jesus had spent a great deal of time, we found ruins of a synagogue and remains of what is thought to be the house of Peter. Only bougainvillea vines and other colorful plants were alive in the city. In Bethsaida, we walked through scenes of ancient destruction—streets of columns, mosaic floors and a large amphitheater. Again the city was deserted.

We sat under the trees in Chorazin, the city where it is believed that Jesus had dinner with Matthew the tax collector, turned follower of Jesus and author of the gospel of Matthew. In the ruins of the third and fourth century Chorazin synagogue (the first century ruins have yet to be found), there was a Moses seat, referred to by Matthew in his gospel. That seat, where the rabbi or other speakers would sit and discuss the Torah must have represented the religious items/trappings of the day and cause Jesus to say, "These people say they honor me, but their hearts are far away." (Matthew 15:8)

The lesson for my heart came at Chorazin where once again it was confirmed that when Jesus predicts that something will happen—it happens! And, rather than merely observing a form of worship, I am reminded daily to love and follow my Lord and to worship Him in spirit and in truth.

# *Canyons*

I worked for many years in a community where employees, upon hire, stated that they had trusted Christ as Savior and intended to serve God through their work. Naturally, we were at all stages in our walk of faith.

It was my hope that every employee would be able to explain simply what it meant to put his/her faith in Christ.

You can imagine the staff's surprise and delight when a former Buddhist staff member offered to explain the following diagram:

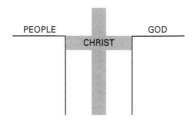

"People on one side of canyon; God on the other side. Because of Jesus on the cross, we can cross over."

"But to all who received him, he gave the right to become children of God. All they needed to do was to trust him to save them." (John 1:12)

"Because of his kindness you have been saved through trusting Christ. And even trusting is not of yourselves; it too is a gift from God. Salvation is not a reward for the good we have done, so none of us can take any credit for it. It is God himself who has made us what we are and given us new lives from Christ Jesus; and long ages ago he planned that we should spend these lives in helping others." (Ephesians 2:8-10)

# Deer

In the middle of the desolate Judean wilderness is the oasis of En Gedi with its lush green foliage, waterfalls, streams and pools of water. To the Hebrew people, the refreshing, living waters of En Gedi were a sign of God's faithfulness to His promises and His life-giving presence in their lives.

The leader on our tour of the Holy Land asked if we would like to make a stop at En Gedi near the Dead Sea. What a meaningful time it was as we observed the deer that still remain in that area, drinking from the streams. Up the hill was the cave in which it is believed that David hid from King Saul and that from this viewpoint David was inspired to write the words: "As the deer pants for water, so I long for you, O God. I thirst for God, the living God." (Psalm 42:1-2a)

Jesus also used the powerful sign of living water in His teaching. It was to a Samaritan woman at Jacob's well that He revealed that He Himself is the Living Water that comes down from heaven and that whoever drinks of this water will never thirst again. (John 4)

Martin J. Nystrom wrote the much-loved praise and worship song, "As The Deer," 1981, Capitol CMG Publishing.* Below is the first stanza and chorus of that song:

As the deer panteth for the water
    So my soul longeth after Thee
You alone are my heart's desire
    And I long to worship Thee.

*Used by permission                                    continued...

(Chorus)
You alone are my strength, my shield
    To You alone may my spirit yield
You alone are my heart's desire
    And I long to worship Thee.

# Mountains

Volcanic snow-covered mountains hold a particular fascination for me. I recall the night I was first mesmerized by one. Several of us were riding home from college for Christmas via White Pass in Washington State. Each turn in the highway gave us a view of the mighty 14,411 foot Mt. Ranier in the moonlight.

While many say that their most common reoccurring dream is of not being ready for a history test, mine is of that mysterious mountain that night.

As a child, believing that help came from God, I couldn't understand the King James translation of Psalm 121:1, "I will lift mine eyes unto the hills, from whence cometh my help." Now I understand that "from whence cometh my help" is not a prepositional phrase, but a question: "Shall I look to the mountain gods for help? No! My help is from Jehovah who made the mountains! And the heavens too!" (Psalm 121:1,2, Living Bible)

For me, every glimpse of those snowy peaks from a ferry, a car window or from my kitchen window causes me to worship the God who made and controls creation.

# Fields

The barley fields of Bethlehem made the story of Ruth in the Old Testament become even more real for me.

The Book of Ruth is a story of crises and ordinary living—famine, leaving home, the death of a spouse, two sons marrying idol worshippers, and the death of those two sons, leaving Naomi with two daughter-in-laws and no grandchildren. We did say, "Crises," didn't we? Naomi's response to all of this was bitterness and a decision to leave Moab where she and her husband and two sons had moved, and return to Bethlehem. Daughter-in-law, Orpha, stayed in Moab, but Ruth quotes the familiar verse: "...Don't make me leave you, for I want to go wherever you go, and to live wherever you live; your people shall be my people, and your God shall be my God." (Ruth 1:16). But this story is also one of finding favor with God and man. In Bethlehem, Naomi had a relative, Boaz, who was a rich land owner. Ruth worked in his fields, picking up the grain left behind by the harvesters.

Whatever she did, she was a stand-out, causing Boaz to ask, "... Hey, who's that girl over there?" (Ruth 2:5b). What a story of Human Resources principles for employees and managers! First, Ruth had a work ethic. It says she started early in the morning and was still at it in the evening—except for taking her breaks (and that was before breaks were the law!). Boaz saw her sitting in the shade of a tree. Boaz told the workers to leave extra barley in the fields—making it easy for Ruth at work. Then, as if this manager hadn't already done enough for her—he builds her up by talking about her reputation in town—of her kindness to her mother-in-law, Naomi. Boaz then, gives Ruth a blessing: "May the Lord God of Israel, under whose wings you have come to take refuge, bless

*continued...*

you for it." (Ruth 2:12). Naomi who was so bitter before, is now so positive! I can't help thinking it was because Ruth was coming home each day, telling of all the blessings at work. Now, Naomi is recognizing the cup half full rather than half empty. To Ruth, she says, "God is blessing us!" Ruth lived God's principles at home, too. She stayed with Naomi and didn't move in with Boaz as soon as she met him. What a story of kindness, good relationships and blessing! The whole fam-damily (spellcheck didn't like that word) is blessed!

Ruth gets a husband, Naomi and Ruth arranged for Boaz to get Naomi's husband's estate, Naomi's going to get a grandchild after all and they're all blessed with heritage when Ruth and Boaz had Obed and Obed had Jesse and Jesse had David (you know where this is going, don't you?) and from David's line came Jesus, our Savior!

# Buildings

In 1936, the French government informed Dad that if missionaries wanted to remain in that area of French Equatorial Africa, they had to build permanent buildings. Dad, whose experience was in the law office of the Bell Telephone Company in Chicago and as a pastor, had no construction experience, so he and Mother knelt in prayer and read the Scriptures in total dependence on their Lord, as was their pattern throughout life. They were quick to say that when they opened the Bible, they did not expect to point to a verse and do exactly what it said. But, when they did seek encouragement, guidance and strength from its pages at this time, they knew ahead of time that God would do something extraordinary for them. They opened the Bible to II. Chronicles 22:15 and found the promise that God would give wisdom in building with skilled stone masters, carpenters and craftsmen of every kind.

This was all fulfilled as the eight-room brick home was built. With giant handsaws, carpenters sawed the wood from trees in the jungle. Masons cut stones and laid the foundation. Bags of cement were mixed with water. The dirt from anthills, rich with saliva, was perfect for making bricks. The Azandes stomped the mud for days while chanting; then the dirt was set in a wooden mold the size of a shoebox for burning in a kiln. Since 1937 the two missionary homes, a hospital, schoolhouse and chapel still stand as a testimony to God's faithfulness to a man and woman who were utterly dependent on God for every great and small thing in their lives. Our son has enjoyed using this story as a devotional to honor God and to honor his heritage.

*continued...*

"I will wait for the Lord to help us, though he is hiding now. My only hope is in him." (Isaiah 8:17)

"You are my refuge and my shield, and your promises are my only source of hope." (Psalm 119:114)

# Goats' Milk

In the first term when my parents were due to leave Africa for furlough, they had only one can of powered milk left which they were saving for the long trip out of Africa. Their goats were dried up and a yellow fever scare had prevented them from getting any supplies from the Belgian Congo. My sister and I needed milk as well as the newborn of an Azande mother with septicemia who could not nurse her baby. My mother went to her knees. She opened her Bible to the following words, "And thou shalt have goats' milk enough for thy food, for the food of thy household, and for the maintenance for thy maidens." (Proverbs 27:27, King James).

Mother ran to find my father to tell him, "We're going to have goat's milk!" That afternoon a message came from a merchant at the government post, stating that he had gone up into the Chad and purchased a herd of goats from the Arabs. He was leaving on a trip and wondered if the missionaries could use the milk from his herd during his absence. The merchant returned just as my family was scheduled to leave for the east coast of Africa and the Indian Ocean.

# Rivers

I took the class in Hope 101 by watching my parents as they trusted a faithful God while working as missionaries in an isolated, disease-laden and primitive part of Africa. My parents were by no means perfect parents, but they did the big things right.

It seemed that every time we got to the river border of Belgian Congo and French Equatorial Africa, we were told that we could not cross because of a quarantine or for some other reason. My parents never argued with the officials. I saw them fall to their knees on their kneeling bench--the running board of our truck. The first words I always heard were: "Lord, You're our only hope!" Each time we were allowed to cross over the crocodile-infested river by pontoon. And, in an area where there were no stores, where the soil was extremely poor soil for growing vegetables and we had no chance of raising stock because of sleeping sickness, we never went without three meals a day.

"I will wait for the Lord to help us; though he is hiding now. My only hope is in him." (Isaiah 8:17)

"You are my refuge and my shield and your promises are my only source of hope." (Psalm 119:114)

# Pyramids

In January of 1946, upon our return to Africa, our family spent two weeks in Egypt at Assuit, a Christian orphanage for about 900—many of whom were blind.

While there, some of our trips included riding camelback up to the Sphinx and the Pyramids. At that time, tourists were allowed to go inside the largest pyramid—the tomb of King Cheops. A guide struck a magnesium strip to light the way as we ascended the ramp. Only my brother, age 6, and I, age 7, could stand straight up on the ramp. My sister and parents had to bend over as we climbed the ramp with the metal slats.

That was my first experience with a pyramid. Most recently, I have appreciated Abraham Maslow's Hierarchy of Needs, published in the American Psychological Review, Volume 50, July 1943, which many students have studied at various levels of their education. The five levels of human need were placed on a pyramid. The bottom, first level was Physiological Needs--the widest level, indicating how so much of life is taken up with the basics for survival (food, water, oxygen, elimination, pH, etc.) as infants and even as adults. The second level was Safety & Security Needs; the third level, Love & Belonging Needs; the fourth level, Self-Esteem Needs—leading to the top level of the pyramid which is Self-Actualization, or "Fulfillment" as I like to think of it.

In leading a large community of residents and their advocates, as well as staff members, my goal was to turn that pyramid upside down. It was hoped that with good customer service, people could live lives that focused less on the basics for existence, to lives that experienced joy and purpose—leading to fulfillment. By

*continued...*

volunteering, writing their life stories, strengthening relationships and assuring that their life issues and documents were in order, residents expressed that they experienced fulfillment.

# *Rainbows*

With my feet up on the window sill and a cup of rich coffee in hand, I looked out over the glassy, deep waters of Lake Chelan in Eastern Washington at sunrise.

Good weather clouds in the blue sky above announced the weather for the day ahead. For a full hour I watched the sprinklers that had been activated to water the grass that sloped down to the water's edge.

I had anticipated enjoying the lake, the sky and the birds, but the surprise was a rainbow that kept appearing each time two dancing sprinklers crossed in the sunlight. Who can see those royal prism colors without thinking of the word, "Promise?"

It has been said there are about 7000 promises in the Bible. I thought of a different one of those 7000 each time the rainbow appeared.

When the Living Bible, by Tyndale House Publishers, 1971, was published, I read through that entire paraphrase of the Scriptures. So captivated was I with the words, that I read through it again—this time writing down every principle, every promise and every verse about the Living God of the Living Bible. As one can imagine it was quite a lengthy manuscript! I was struck by the correlation of the principles to be lived if I were to enjoy the accompanying promises and the presence of the Living God.

"Be delighted with the Lord. Then he will give you all your heart's desires." (Psalm 37:4)

*continued...*

"In everything you do, put God first and he will direct you and crown your efforts with success." (Proverbs 3:6)

"But they that wait upon the Lord shall renew their strength. They shall mount up with wings like eagles; they shall run and not be weary; they shall walk and not faint." (Isaiah 40:31)

"Come to me and I will give you rest..." (Matthew 11:28)

"...anyone who believes in him shall not perish but have eternal life." (John 3:16)

# Fountain of Joy

Looking through a box of books that had belonged to my parents, I came across a baby book for my brother, Jimmy, who died of pneumonia and malaria at age 15 months. It was during my parents' first term at Zemio in the colony that was then, French Equatorial Africa, that my brother died. I read of his birth date in the mud house, his measurements and the baby clothes that had arrived from America from family and friends. I sobbed when I got to the page where Mother recorded how she had to dress her little son for burial and how my father placed him in a trunk and then led the burial service in PaZande and also in French for the French official who lived at the nearby post. The grief was overwhelming as they experienced this while isolated from family, friends and their home church members. Yet, the story we as remaining children heard all our lives from them was that both my mother and my father were given the gift of unexplainable joy from God in the middle of their grief.

My sister who was age two and a half at the time, clearly remembers coming home down the dirt path to the mud house following the service. She says, "To this day, I am profoundly touched that even in this time of grieving, my parents had true joy and great tranquility because of the honor they afforded the Word of God." Several hundred Azande people came from many miles around, having heard the message, "Bwana's son has died," by drumbeat from village to village. More Africans received Christ at that time than at any other time in my parents' ministry when they saw the joy, peace and hope of heaven in the lives of my parents.

"What a wonderful God we have—he is the Father of our Lord, Jesus Christ, the source of every mercy and the one who so

*continued...*

wonderfully comforts and strengthens us in our hardships
and trials.  And why does he do this?  So that when others are
troubled, needing our sympathy and encouragement, we can pass
on to them this same help and comfort God has given us."
(II. Corinthians 1:3,4)

# Family Records

Frequently I was asked by Journalism students or children wishing to earn community service hours, if they could visit with senior residents to get their stories. It seemed so much more profitable to have children of all ages meet face-to-face with people of another generation, than to have them weed the garden for service hours!

An interview form was given to them to keep the information chronologically correct and to get answers to questions over the resident's life span.

When my own grandchildren interviewed residents, using these interview questions, they were not as taken with the fact that the resident was born in Kansas, as to the answers to the following questions:

What difficult thing did you face and how did you survive it?
What do you want to be said about your life?
What advice do you have for me or for friends my age?

I felt that next to giving opportunities for growth in Christ, there was nothing more important than getting residents that I worked with to record their stories of faith, romance, patriotism and humor—whether in a two-page story or in a life-story. A notebook of their first 68 short stories remains by the fireplace in that community for all to enjoy.

Once when a 90-year old gentleman in the Independent Living setting pulled his emergency cord, I responded to his call. After assessing that he was medically stable, I asked him if the picture over his bed of an old building on a prairie, was of significance.

*continued...*

He said, "That was my first parsonage in North Dakota." I asked if his children knew that. He said he didn't think they would be interested. Regardless, we marked the back of the framed picture. This man wrote his entire life story before he died. Wondering whether it was really worth the time to encourage residents to record their life stories and mark their photos, I phoned his son in Oregon and his daughter in North Dakota after their father's death and asked them if the record he had left had meaning for them. They said it meant everything to them.

# Family Tree

I was hooked on genealogy the day I found details about my
grandfather on the back of an old photograph. Since that time
it has been a marvelous adventure learning how to search for
information, finding living descendants in the U.S. and abroad
and leading Genealogy 101 classes to get others interested in
searching for their roots.

Alex Haley also helped spark an interest for many of us in
finding our roots when he authored the book, *Roots,* published by
Doubleday in 1976.

A lady in the Independent Living setting of the Senior Living
Community was in Hospice. She and her daughter were quite
distressed as they sat in her apartment thinking of what they should
be doing in their last days together.

I asked if the names were on the back of all the photographs. The
daughter pulled photos off the wall to be labeled and then asked
her mother to identify who was in the photos of the prints that
were in a box.

Next, I asked for any names, dates, places and stories that the mother
could record for her son, daughter and future generations. With
the information, I searched all weekend for records for their family
tree. On Sunday afternoon, I returned with census records that had
the resident listed as a girl of six; then of 16, plus other records that
made her feel rooted and could be left to her descendants.

If I have any regret about my own dad, it is that I did not give
him the pleasure of my being interested in what he told me about

*continued...*

his ancestors. I had to learn the hard way the name of my great grandparents, the towns in Germany and in Switzerland from which they came, etc. However, I feel I have now honored him by finding so much ancestral information and by visiting descendants in the U.S. and abroad.

# People Favored by God and Man

The dictionary uses a good part of a page in defining the word, "Favor." Favor is a gracious, kind or friendly attitude; an act of kindness; an act requiring sacrifice or special generosity (as God has favored us!); to hold in high regard; regarded with approval; to be in support of; indulged.

Most of my favorite characters in the Bible, and possibly, your favorites too, are people described as being favored by God and man.

Statements like these were made about Joseph who had lived God's principles consistently in a foreign land: "He was a man filled with the Spirit of God." Pharoah said: "Who could do it better than Joseph?" He was put in charge of the complete famine project/was made second in command in the land of Egypt. He found favor with God and man.

Ruth was a widow/a single person who made good choices. She put aside her personal desires and stayed with her mother-in-law instead of moving in with Boaz whom she had met. She had a good work ethic and was known for the love and kindness she showed others. She lived God's principles and took refuge under God's wings—now that is a favored spot! She found favor with God and favor with man—Boaz, whom she married.

Samuel was a boy who not only grew taller, but obeyed and had a heart towards God. It was said of him that he was a favorite of God and became everyone's favorite.

*continued...*

It was said of David, in I. Samuel that the Lord was with David. He was a man after God's own heart. He was favored by God and was immensely popular with the people.

Esther was a young lady with a destiny to save a nation at great risk to her own life. She was favored by God in being chosen to be queen and favored by man when King Ahasuerus was delighted with her and placed a crown on her head.

Daniel was a teenager taken from his home, to a foreign land. When he and his friends were tempted by the king to eat food that he was not to eat, he wisely gave a creative alternative and was later found to be healthier than all the others who had eaten the food ordered by the king. It was said of Daniel and his three friends, "God gave these four youths great ability to learn and they soon mastered all the literature and science of the time, and God gave to Daniel special ability in understanding the meanings of dreams and visions." (Daniel 1:17). The four youths were put on the king's staff of advisors. Daniel praised the God of heaven, saying, "Blessed be the name of God forever and ever, for he alone has all wisdom and all power. World events are under his control..." (Daniel 2:20, 21b). Isn't that encouraging for our lives today? Daniel found favor with God and man.

We read that Mary's friend, Elizabeth said to Mary, the mother of Jesus, "You are favored by God above all other women, and your child is destined for God's mightiest praise. (Luke 1:42a). "You believed that God would do what he said; that is why he has given you this wonderful blessing." (Luke 1:45). This is the same reason why Joseph, Ruth, Samuel, David, Esther and Daniel were honored! Mary's reply shows she knew Bible doctrine and already had faith in her Son that was to be born. "Oh, how I praise the Lord. How I rejoice in God my Savior! For he took notice of his lowly servant girl, and now generation after generation forever shall call me blest of God. For he, the mighty Holy One, has done great things to me. His mercy goes on from generation to generation, to all who reverence him. How powerful is his mighty

*continued...*

arm! How he scatters the proud and haughty ones! He has torn princes from their thrones and exalted the lowly. He has satisfied the hungry hearts and sent the rich away with empty hands. And how he has helped his servant, Israel! He has not forgotten his promise to be merciful. For he promised our fathers—Abraham and his children—to be merciful to them forever." (Luke 1:46b-55). Well, don't you think He favored the right girl?

The supreme example of finding favor with God and man is in Jesus Christ. "And Jesus increased in wisdom, and stature, and in favor with God and man." (Luke 2:52, King James). This verse is usually used to remind us that we, like Jesus, should grow in wisdom (mentally/emotionally); in stature (physically) and in favor with God (spiritually) and man (socially). Christ could have had every reason to have people not like Him. He called them "sinners," "hypocrites," and said He was the <u>only</u> Way, the <u>only</u> Truth and the <u>only</u> Life. Yet, there must have been something about the way He said it that resulted in not only finding favor with God, but finding favor with man as well.

"May the Lord bless and protect <u>you</u>; may the Lord's face radiate with joy because of <u>you</u>; may he be gracious to <u>you</u>, show <u>you</u> his favor, and give <u>you</u> his peace." (Numbers 6:24)

# Neighbors

When we moved into a new home we had built, it was not comfortable interacting with our next door neighbors, related to building heights and boundary lines. This unpleasantness continued until we attended a seminar in which the question was posed: "Is there anyone who would not want to become a Christian because of you?" Surmising that would be true of these neighbors, I went next door to borrow an onion (a bit more original than borrowing a cup of sugar, don't you think?). While there I said, "I want to ask forgiveness for any hard feelings I/we may have caused between our families." Immediately the neighbor invited me in for coffee. The next Sunday morning her husband asked us where we attended church. Their whole family attended the week-long seminar that we had attended annually for many years. Our hearts were deeply moved when we saw their entire family raise their hands to indicate they wished to receive Christ as Savior. They found a wonderful church where they served as elders, led home Bible Study groups and were involved in Christian Education. Several years later we attended the Christ-honoring memorial service that their adult children planned for the mother and father who were killed in an auto accident. Those parents' children and grandchildren continue to honor and serve Christ.

# Friends

The best neighbor I ever had was a lady whose two sons and our son loved to play together. I had held a Five-Day Good News Club at our home and both of her sons had prayed to receive Christ as Savior. Wanting to let my friend know of her sons' decisions, I went to her home with Campus Crusade for Christ's "Four Spiritual Laws" booklet. Law I said, "God loves you and has a wonderful plan for your life." When I got to Law II which said, "Man is sinful and separated from God..." my friend jumped up and said, "There is no such thing as sin!" Quickly, I said, "I guess you are not ready to talk about this now." We continued as friends and one day this very talented seamstress was having difficulty getting a zipper into the slippery material of a bridesmaid's dress. She turned to me and said, "Pray that I'll get this zipper in right this time." I said, "Don't ask me to pray! I had asked God to make you miserable on your trip to Las Vegas with your husband and you said you had a ball!" She laughed and said, "Actually, we did not have a good time and were not holding hands on the street corners there, but when you invited us to the Billy Graham Crusade in Seattle, my husband and I were holding hands on the way out of the stadium." This delightful person is strong in faith and will always be my favorite neighbor.

# Cracks

Life's Landscape Lessons keep coming to me. The other day I parked in a grocery store parking lot. In front of me was a vacant building. The empty windows reflected light from the sun in the sky above. But it was the crack in a broken pane that caught my attention. From it was a blaze of refractory sunlight that reminded me of the verse, "But we have this treasure in earthen vessels, that the excellency of the power may be of God, and not of us." (II Corinthians 4:7, King James). A friend once reminded me that the treasure of Christ has been placed inside us, the clay pots, by the Potter. We do not have to be perfect pots for the treasure to be seen. A watching world can see the treasure inside even better through the cracks.

II. Corinthians 4:7-9, Living Bible, says it this way: "But this precious treasure—this light and power that now shine within us—is held in a perishable container, that is, in our weak bodies. Everyone can see that the glorious power within must be from God and is not our own. We are pressed on every side by troubles, but not crushed and broken. We are perplexed because we don't know why things happen as they do, but we don't give up and quit. We are hunted down, but God never abandons us. We get knocked down, but we get up and keep going."

# *Bowing*

I recall receiving Christ as my Savior at age four. When my parents
returned from Africa to the U.S., Mother had a Good News
Club in our home and I prayed to invite Christ into my life after
hearing the story of the Good Shepherd in the Gospel of John.
Not everyone can recall a particular time they received Christ.
What is important for us to know is that though we were once
spiritually blind, now we see.

It has been said that Christians are people who bow twice—once in
recognition of the need of a Savior and then, in gratitude for the
rest of our lives for what He continues to do for us.

Think about a word. It's not a pretty word—in fact, it might not be
a word at all. It is, "WOW!" My husband and I went to a concert
where we heard a gentleman sing a song that he wrote about his
father, titled, "WOW!" When his elderly father came to live with
him, he said, "WOW!" when a bowl of cereal was placed in front
of him at breakfast. At lunch, he said, "WOW!" when given a bowl
of soup. There was another, "WOW!" when a modest supper was
placed in front of him. And, when he was dying, he opened his
eyes and looked up. Whatever he saw, caused him to say, "WOW!"

May we, like this man, spend our lives bowing in gratitude for all
we have been given. WOW!

I dedicate

*Life's Landscape Lessons*

to my three grandchildren,

Michael,

Kaley,

Emma,

for whom I have written

the following poems.

# Rocks — Michael James Kenyon Rocks!

It started out with Rock-a-Bye, Baby after your proud parents brought you home from the hospital.

And, as a baby your mom held you while boating to rocky beaches in the San Juan Islands and camping at Lincoln Rock.

In no time you were a toddler, picking up rocks, stashing them into your pockets, then into your drawers.

A photo of you with stick in one hand and rock in the other, watching little sis leaning over to pick a dandelion, won the Editor's Award in a contest, with the title, "Who Needs Toys, Little Sister?"

One of your first words was "work-a-man" excitedly said each time you saw workers blasting rocks on your way to Lake Chelan where your dad taught you to fish from the rocks below the condo.

You too, have always been a "work-a-man"—wowing customers with your work ethic while beautifying lawns and rockeries.

And, you were the rock for your soccer team—winning the sportsmanship award and the state championship trophy for King's High, while your family and grandparents, as always, cheered from the stands.

*continued...*

With expertise and with digital camera in hand, you captured the ancient rock walls of England's Windsor Castle and France's Notre Dame Cathedral.

Your immaculate trucks are loaded with all the extras, including your favorite rock music.

Now, you're studying business construction. Just as you know a house must be built on a firm foundation, may you always remember that a wise man builds his life on The Rock.

"The Lord is a strong rock; the godly run to Him and are safe." Proverbs 18:10

Michael, keep ROCKING!

# Birthdays of Kaley Nichole

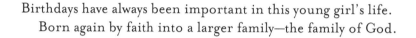

"It's a girl" were the first words she heard—
   the same words that made her mom and
   dad ecstatic
      and grandparents delighted.

No need to say, "Smile" for the camera
that captured
   the little family, now joined by brother in birthing room bed.

Birthdays have always been important in this young girl's life.
   Born again by faith into a larger family—the family of God.

Dress-up parties with friends at three,
   Beach parties with waves spilling on the sand,
      Cheerleading parades,

Hopping up on stage in Maui each time there was a call
   for those celebrating something!

Dinner cruise past the Eiffel Tower that treated a fourteen year old
   to cuisine, entertainment and views to last a lifetime.

Driving with ease at fifteen.

Soon she'll be called, "Sweet Sixteen."
   Whoever created that title must have had Kaley in mind—
      Volunteering so well with children,
      Keeping good friends and seeking new,
      Making every garment in the store look good,
      Celebrating with teammates every effort that goes into
      playing so well.

*"Lord, please keep this beautiful girl that You and I love so dearly*
*Close to You all the birthdays and in-between days of her life."*

## Stage of Life —
## Presenting
## Emma Alexandra

"Meet little Emma," were the
first words we heard
    As you were ushered from
    your dressing room to a
    waiting world.

With perfect rosebud mouth and eyes so big and blue,
    This little star woke up each day to constant rave reviews.

Backstage your mom and dad have directed so superbly,
    Assisted by the stagehands who worship the ground you walk on.

Before age two you entertained with animated dancing,
    Using words like, "anticipate" and counting up to 30.

You lifted our eyes when your sweet voice said, "See moon,"
    Our minds were wowed with your "reading," complete with title
    and author.

You helped fill our senses as together we smelled each flower,
    We stopped to listen as you asked, "From where is the music
    coming?"

So, as you live and act each day upon that grand old stage of life,
    May you win the highest award of all, "Approved Unto God."

And from that front row balcony or that reserved box seat in heaven,
    Grandma will be wildly cheering for Emma Alexandra.

Made in the USA
San Bernardino, CA
19 November 2015